THIS BOOK BELONGS TO

HILDA WILLIAMS.

SOLD FOR A FARTHING

The Daily Reading

SOLD FOR A FARTHING

by

CLARE KIPPS

Photographic Illustrations by Kenneth Gamm

FREDERICK MULLER LIMITED
LONDON

FIRST PUBLISHED BY FREDERICK MULLER LTD.
AND PRINTED IN GREAT BRITAIN BY
BESLEY AND COPP LTD.
EXETER
BOUND BY THE DORSTEL PRESS LTD., HARLOW

First Impression, September, 1953
Second Impression, October, 1953
Third Impression, December, 1953
Fourth Impression, December, 1953
Fifth Impression, December, 1953
Sixth Impression, May, 1954
Seventh Impression, October, 1954

CONTENTS

—

ILLUSTRATIONS

Acknowledgments are due to Nancy Price for her generous sponsorship of this little book and for giving it the name by which it is known.

" Atheists naturally regard the co-existence of man and the other animals as a mere contingent result of interacting biological facts ; and the taming of an animal by man as a purely arbitrary interference of one species with another. The ' real ' or ' natural ' animal to them is the wild one, and the tame animal is an artificial or unnatural thing. But a Christian must not think so. Man was appointed by God to have dominion over the beasts, and everything he does to an animal is either a lawful exercise, or a sacrilegious abuse, of an authority by divine right. The ' tame ' animal is therefore, in the deepest sense, the only natural one.

More animals than you might expect are ready to adore man if they are given a reasonable opportunity ; for man was made to be the priest and even, in one sense, the Christ of the animals—the mediator through whom they apprehend so much of the Divine splendour as their irrational nature allows."

———

" From *The Problem of Pain* by C. S. Lewis (Geoffrey Bles Ltd.) "

FOREWORD

by

JULIAN HUXLEY

The true student will also be a lover of birds ; and the true lover of birds will also inevitably become their student. To all such bird-students and bird-lovers, Mrs. Kipps' book will give much interest and pleasure.

In the first place, it is a remarkable and I believe a unique achievement to rear and keep alive a helpless sparrow fledgling less than a day old, not merely to maturity but until it died of old age. It is probable that very few wild birds ever reach old age, and that none ever die of it ; even captive birds generally succumb to some disease or to some dysfunction due to their abnormal food and conditions of life. Thus it is of considerable scientific interest to know that this particular house-sparrow did die of old age, and that he lived for 12 years, 7 weeks and 4 days.

The details of his ageing are also interesting. He seems to have reached the highest pitch of physical appearance, beauty of plumage, intelligence, and vocalizing capacity between the ages of 4 and 6. He enjoyed excellent health until soon after his 11th birthday, when he would sometimes fall off his perch during the night and have occasional attacks that Mrs. Kipps describes as hysteria ; shortly afterwards he suffered a kind of stroke, during which he became unconscious, resulting in partial paralysis.

After this, he never sang again, and failed rapidly in strength and agility, finding great difficulty in climbing to his perch, suffered from constipation, and began shedding his feathers. M. and B. cured the constipation, champagne pepped him up, and a special vitamin-rich diet improved his general health. But he still showed a marked lack of motor co-ordination, and was constantly falling on his back and having to be picked up. It is remarkable to learn that after a time he spontaneously discovered how to right himself, by somersaulting from his inverted position and landing right way up. Gradually he lost interest in most of the things and events that had previously stimulated him. Eventually he became unable either to perch or fly, and had to be constantly tended and kept clean. However, his behaviour still continued remarkably adaptable ; and when provided with a soft padded floor to obviate bumps and injuries from falling, he invented the sport of jumping to and fro with some object held in his beak, and the game of throwing it up and retrieving it.

His left foot had always been deformed ; but now his lack of motor co-ordination prompted him to use it to steady his food-container while he ate ; and his success in this led him to use the other foot also for the same purpose. Most curious of all, when, after a heart-attack later in his 12th year, he found hopping too great an exertion, he learnt to walk, using his feet alternately— something quite unheard of in a normal sparrow.

For a few weeks he practised food-hoarding for the first time in his life, but then gave up the habit altogether. His sleep became deeper, he slept longer, and fell asleep more readily. He evinced a great partiality for a hairpin, and would sit with it held in his beak, or laid before him at the entrance to the ' tent ' in which he slept. His hearing remained acute, but his sight progressively failed until he was nearly blind. On the last day of his life he was too weak to stand, and lay motionless in Mrs. Kipps' hand for several hours. Suddenly he lifted his head, gave a call and died.

* * * * *

The most unexpected fact in the book is the sparrow's song. Wild house-sparrows have nothing that can be called a song, merely a series of chirps and calls. Thus it is really very extra-ordinary that this bird should, quite spontaneously and without any deliberate teaching, have started to sing. Presumably the unusual sounds with which he found himself surrounded stimulated him to unusual vocalizations; for during the first few months of his life he had achieved a vocabulary of notes and calls a good deal more extensive than that of wild sparrows, and was continually adding to his repertoire. And Mrs. Kipps records his obvious excitement when she played the piano. But it was a complete surprise when she found that he had started (in solitude) a true song, with a melodic line, high notes, and even trills.

Mrs. Kipps had been a professional musician, and endeavoured to keep up her piano practice, even when she was an Air-Raid Warden during the blitz. It is possible, as she tentatively suggests, that without this regular musical stimulus, the sparrow would never have developed a song; but we cannot be sure. In any case, the development was a spontaneous one : no attempt was made to try to teach him to sing, and his song was not in any sense an imitation of what he heard on the piano.

His full song developed only during the spring and summer of the year after he was hatched, when his reproductive organs had ripened and were pouring their hormones into his blood. This was to be expected : what was unexpected was that he should develop any song at all. Playing the piano would usually serve as a stimulus for him to begin singing : " music that trilled and scales played rapidly in the treble " seemed to affect him most powerfully.

It is of further interest that he developed two very distinct songs. These were sometimes sung separately, though usually the simpler served as introduction to the more elaborate one, which included two eight-note trills. Of course many songbirds, like the Nightingale and the Throstle, have a repertoire of several distinct song-phrases, but these are hardly ever given singly, and are rarely so different that they could be mistaken for the productions of two different kinds of bird, as often happened with this sparrow. In fact I can only think of one wild British species with two radically distinct songs—the Wood Warbler : but here the two songs are always given separately, never with one serving as introduction to the other.

Further points of interest are that he sang all the year round except during the moult ; that at the end of his 5th year he gave up the second trill in his second song, in favour of a harsh croak ; that when a Hartz Mountain Roller Canary was kept in the same room, its singing had not the slightest effect on the sparrow's song (it is possible, in the light of Poulsen's work on Chaffinches, that something of the Canary's song would have been " imprinted " on the sparrow if the experiment had been made in the sparrow's first spring after fledging) ; and that, as already mentioned, he entirely ceased to sing after the paralytic stroke in the last year of his life.

* * * * *

As was to be expected, the sparrow accepted Mrs. Kipps as its parent, at least for most purposes. Whether this was effected by an early, sudden, and once-for-all acceptance, as occurs in the so-called " imprinting " of goslings described by Konsad Lorenz, or was gradually " learnt," it is difficult to be sure, though the absence of any reaction to his own reflection in a mirror, which in most sexually dimorphic bird species is normally taken to be a rival, and accordingly treated with hostility, speaks in favour of imprinting, or at least of some drastic and irreversible change in the birds' instinctive behaviour-mechanisms. In any event the transference to the unnatural parent-object seems to have been effective from an early age. When still quite young, he fought in defence of his right of access to his mistress and to his ' nest ' in her bed ; and when adult, he regularly ' displayed ' to her, and never to any other organisms, whether other human beings, wild birds of his own or other species, or a tame canary that for a time shared his room.

It is of considerable interest that, even quite late in life, he would " forget " his mistress if she were absent for over a week, standing and staring in a confused way for sometime before showing signs of recognition. It is clear that he recognized her as an individual : on one occasion when a friend (a woman Doctor) came to stay the night when Mrs. Kipps was away, the sparrow was furious, and when she got into bed, attacked her so violently that she was obliged to get up and wait until the sparrow had taken his accustomed place !

When, at 4 years old, his cage was moved close to a window, he would react to the calls of wild sparrows by flying towards the fanlight and calling himself, and he became excited at the sight of their typical sexual scuffles (group fights and displays) ; but otherwise he evinced no interest in them, even when they came into the room.

On the other hand, the sight of their activities in the outer world seems to have taught him fear. Previously, in his first autumn, he had shown no fear (merely immobilized surprise or interest) at a cat glaring at him from just outside his cage ; but now the sight of a distant cat (and, curiously enough, even more the sight of the window-cleaner) threw him into a panic. At this time, possibly also through watching the wild birds, he first began catching flies on the window-pane.

As a result of this transference of his main interest to Mrs. Kipps, the sparrow developed substitute goals for various of his instinctive activities. A place under the eiderdown in his mistress' bed speedily became one of his substitute nests, the other being inside her jumper. It is noteworthy that he never fouled his substitute nests, crawling to the rim of the basin, for instance, to project his excreta over the edge. When he became sexually mature, the nesting-place under the eiderdown seemed to acquire significance as a breeding nest, and he would bring match-sticks or hair-pins into it. However, he never attempted any serious nest-building, even when provided with suitable material.

Mrs. Kipps' hair provided him with a substitute outlet for his dusting instinct, and he habitually indulged in imaginary dust-baths in it. Sometimes he would do the same in, or rather on, the front page of the *Times*, and once attempted to pick up the letters one by one, and to put them under his wings : this extraordinary action was apparently a substitute for " anting," that curious activity of many birds who pick up ants and put them under their wings, possibly to get rid of parasites.

Mrs. Kipps' records a number of other remarkable facts, but I have said enough to show that her book contains much of scientific interest. But it has also a general appeal, both in the account of Mrs. Kipps' patient devotion to her sparrow, and in the many details, often unexpected and fascinating, of the sparrow's behaviour and individuality. I have much enjoyed reading it, and I am sure that a wide public will share that enjoyment.

JULIAN HUXLEY,

May, 1953.

PROLOGUE

———

I have often been asked, even by people as illustrious as Walter de la Mare, to write an exact account of the life of my sparrow. I have hesitated to do so for fear of inducing others to keep so engaging a creature in captivity—I do not think that wild birds should be deprived of their liberty.

Now that I am committed to the task, however, I have taken infinite pains to make this little book a faithful record and to avoid exaggeration—knowing full well that only thus can it be of any value. What may at first seem over-imaginative in my interpretation of the behaviour of this little bird is at least the result of studied observation ; and whenever I have felt uncertain as to whether his actions were due to chance, instinct or intelligence, I have left it to readers to decide.

I have chosen a simple narrative form, without any pretension to literary style, as the safest vehicle of the unadorned and sober truth. Only in a few circumstantial details, which are of no importance, have I departed in any way from actual fact. The little bird was not bombed from his nest as was generally believed. He was one of prodigal Nature's many casualties, and was probably flung out because he was faulty in foot and wing and would stand no chance of survival.

The photographs were all taken after his catastrophic and all-but-fatal illness, when he was nearly twelve years old, showing the draggled wings and dilapidated tail, and I much regret that I did not secure some pictures earlier that would have done justice to him when he was in his prime. It is a strange fact that, though in no single instance was he posed or coaxed into position, he assumed spontaneously the attitude, mood and expression demanded by the illustration.

I have always been a lover of birds. It is a curious fact, though in every case it may have been mere coincidence, that an unusual appearance of one of these mysterious and exquisite beings has always heralded an event of great importance in my life. When I was born, a magpie pecked three times on the window as the nurse announced that a puny and insignificant infant was a girl. My mother took it as an ill omen—for she had a strange horror of magpies—and she died within three days. But neither magpie nor raven has ever been to me a harbinger of sorrow. I have had friends among the wild songsters and have been on nodding terms with a nightingale, but no bird has ever been so constant and beloved a companion as my little house sparrow.

This is the story—not of a pet, but of an intimate friendship, extending over many years, between a human being and a bird. As I am a widow, living in solitude and comparative seclusion, perhaps no sparrow has ever been privileged to enjoy (or to endure) such exclusive human companionship, and it may throw new light on the habits, temperament and possibilities of one of the most interesting and adaptable of all birds.

To quote, with his kind permission, from a criticism of this book by Walter de la Mare in a personal letter to me : " It is all but unique. From what I have already seen of it the Sparrow's Biography will be a little gem and the photographs are astonishing in themselves and a wonderful witness to the love that extends to all creatures great and small. What a marvel of insight he gives to anyone with a groatsworth of imagination. One asks oneself how *could* that languageless (or all but languageless) morsel of feathers have loved anything so dearly as he loved his human friend. But mysteries begin to *abound* at this point— and by ' that friend ' I meant of course also the Angel Gabriel."

CHAPTER ONE

THE FOUNDLING

July the first, nineteen hundred and forty, if I can trust my memory, was a dull and somewhat chilly day for the time of year, especially a year that was to become so famous in history for its cloudless noons. The Phoney War had been followed by cataclysmic events on the Continent of Europe, but so far our own country had remained mysteriously free from interference by the enemy. All through the bitter months of a hard winter we had tramped the ice-bound streets and waited in the eerie silence of the black-out for the bombs that never fell. This period of calm, though we did not know it at the time, was soon to develop into the furious onslaught of the Blitzkrieg, but the duty of the Civil Defence—or the A.R.P. Service as it was then called—was to be vigilant and wait.

I was returning from a long day's duty as an Air-Raid Warden at a neighbouring Post when I saw, on the doorstep of my little bungalow in one of London's suburbs, a tiny bird that had fallen or been thrown from its nest. It appeared to be newly-hatched, probably within the last few hours, and was naked, blind, goggle-eyed and apparently lifeless.

Feeling that if a new-born infant is left outside one's doorstep something should be done about it, I picked it up, wrapped it in warm flannel and, sitting over the kitchen fire, endeavoured for several hours to revive it. After I had succeeded in opening its soft beak—an operation that required a delicate touch and immense patience to avoid injury—I propped it open with a spent match and dripped one drop of warm milk every few minutes down the little throat. At the end of half-an-hour, though the bird was still quite cold, I noticed a slight movement of one skinny wing, so, after adding a little soaked bread to the last feed, I put it gently into a small pudding-basin lined and covered with wool, which I deposited in the airing-cupboard. Then, fully expecting it to die in the night, I went to bed.

To my astonishment, early next morning I heard a faint, continuous sound coming from that airing-cupboard—an incredibly thin yet happy sound, the kind of noise a pin would make if it could sing; and there was the little creature, still in his porcelain cradle, but warm and alert and crying for his breakfast.

After that his mouth was rarely shut; and, as he required constant feeding, I took him with me in his basin to the Warden's Post, where he began to serve his country by providing us with endless amusement during the long hours of waiting. I fed him on soaked bread mixed with Bemax, hard-boiled yolk of egg, and one drop of halibut-liver oil, given frequently in small quantities and pushed gently down his throat with the carefully-pointed end of a match. Though the children of the neighbourhood constantly brought along caterpillars and worms in matchboxes tied with blue ribbon, I kept him strictly to this vegetarian diet; and he thrived and grew into a lusty and importunate fledgling.

On the third day a slit appeared in the middle of each of his goggle-eyes, and gradually he opened them on to my large, featherless face and perchlike fingers, and began to look around him. As he had never seen a bird I suppose he accepted me without question as his natural guardian. When his feathers— which seemed to grow mostly at night—began to cover his little body, and the hot cupboard was no longer necessary, he slept in an old fur glove on my pillow, waking me at dawn for his first feed by chirping loudly and pulling my hair.

My intention of course had been to set him free as soon as he could fly and feed himself, but as the wing-feathers developed, a tragedy was revealed, and it looked as though he would never be able to fly freely or to any height that would be reasonably safe. The left wing appeared to be normal, but the right was obviously deformed, the primary feathers standing upright above his back like a little fan. It had a curious effect, this fan-wing, particularly when he fluttered it at my approach in the most engaging manner. However, he learned to jump and to use his wings, in the manner of fledglings, to help his feet as he scrambled after me from room to room. The left foot was also faulty and had a deformed and curled hind toe.

As soon as he was able to feed himself I left him at home, shut safely into a small room with food and milk in each corner of the floor. He soon began to recognise my voice and step, and even the sound of my key in the door, and gave me a vociferous welcome on my return. The moment I opened the door of his boudoir there would be a rush of flying feet, and he would scramble up my leg, over my knee and on to my shoulder, chattering excitedly, before tucking himself under my chin or just inside my collar.

My bed, though, was his heaven, and to snuggle under the eiderdown with me his idea of supreme bliss. It has been so all his life, and here I might mention what is surely an interesting fact. As soon as he had outgrown the complete helplessness of infancy, and long before he was fully-fledged, he began to regard his resting-place as something to be kept clean and he never made anything dirty that served him as a nest. He would struggle up to the top of his wool-lined basin, perch on the rim with his diminutive tail over the edge, and then drop down again for another snooze. When he used my bed as a place in which to sleep, he never fouled it but, if I allowed him to play there, I had to provide him with a washable play-rug. I should imagine it is quite impossible to house-train a sparrow, or any bird for that matter, but some inborn instinct must surely have controlled his behaviour in this respect, and he has never let me down. " A wise bird," says the old adage, " never fouls its own nest."

It was very curious that, while in some respects he was guided so infallibly and so consistently by his natural instincts, he developed habits which seemed to be in direct opposition to them. For instance, so far as I know (and I am quite ready to be corrected by anyone who is better informed than myself), wild birds do not lie on their backs, and if a bird is found in that position I imagine it is fairly safe to assume that it is dead.

But my youngster loved lying on his back, kicking with his feet as a kitten or a baby does; and, as his balance was perfect and he never allowed anyone but myself to see him in such an un-dignified position (at least until he was very old) I am quite sure that it had nothing whatever to do with the malformation of his wing. He often lay thus, looking at me sideways with the most comical expression, as if wondering what sort of bird I could possibly be, or playing with me and pushing away my fingers with his little feet when I tickled him; but in his early days he invariably jumped up with great alacrity at the approach of a stranger. It certainly showed a complete absence of fear when we were alone together and a confidence in me that never once failed him in all the years that followed. In spite of an occasional mishap, as when he fell into the washing-up bowl and had to be lifted out, washed and dried with many complaints on his side, he bore me no ill-will and grew up to regard me as someone who always rescued him from his difficulties and embarrassments.

It was not long before he realised that when my duties com-pelled me to be out all night, I usually lay down on my return to snatch a few hours' sleep. He grew to expect this and, after watching the process of tea-making with great interest and guzzling some milk from a teaspoon, he would lead me to the little bed that had been made on the floor in the safest corner of the room. It was a fantastic sight—worthy of Walt Disney— to watch this tiny creature, his fan-wing fluttering and his little head with its round bright eyes turning sideways to make sure that I was following, lead me with solemn hops and chirpings to my rest. If I undressed first he would sit on the pillow, calling impatiently until I was ready: then, taking care that he did not get hurt as his elephantine bedfellow settled herself in, he would toboggan headlong down the pillow, run right over my face and cuddle down in my neck under the eiderdown. At this moment of ecstacy he always seemed to run rather than hop, though this of course was an illusion. After a few pre-liminary pecks and pinches expressing his dire displeasure when I moved or fidgeted, we would lose consciousness together for several hours.

An amusing incident occurred when I lent my bed to a friend for the night, getting in beside her on my return in the morning. There was a terrible scene, for the little bird considered it an outrage. He ran up and down the pillow, scolding, threatening and then attacking the intruder with such ferocity that she was obliged to get out and stand patiently in a corner while his small majesty took his accustomed place. Only when he was comfortably settled did he graciously permit her to return. She was a doctor, and remarked that, in a life of varied experiences, she had never before been ordered out of bed by a sparrow !

I gradually became bird-conscious, whether awake or asleep, and always moved cautiously for fear of crushing or treading on so small a companion ; but I began to realise that, sooner or later, such complete freedom for him must end in disaster. There were visitors, too, many of whom were children, and *they* were not bird-conscious. Something had to be done before it was too late. I tried him with a small tree, planted in a tub and placed invitingly in a corner of the room, vainly hoping that he would perch there and make it his headquarters, but he fled from it in terror and hid himself down my neck. I hung it with delicacies and tried to persuade him to feed there ; but, wiser than Eve, he couldn't run from it fast enough, and would crouch on the floor, lifting his little wings, as tiny children do their arms, beseeching to be picked up and hidden from this monstrous thing. So, reluctantly enough, I bought a large, roomy cage and, putting the familiar pudding-basin on its floor, I introduced him to it. To my relief and astonishment he went in at once as if he had been bred from generations of cage-birds, and he has loved it, or its successors, ever since.

When I was at home and able to pay sufficient attention to him, the door of this cage was fastened open so that he could go in and out at will, and he always came to me at once. That and my bed—and, of course, my person—were his own private possessions, his estate in defence of which he was prepared to fight with beak and claw, and fight he did, to the intense amusement of any visitors who dared to overstep his boundaries. He took very little interest in anything else in the house and, when left alone in the room, invariably found his way back to his cage. It was amusing to watch his determined and tireless efforts to climb to ever greater heights until, after many tumbles, he could rock triumphantly in his swing with as much pride (in proportion to his ambition) as if he had scaled the summit of Mount Everest. As for me, my legs were his tree-trunks, my fingers his perches and my head his clothes-brush. He enjoyed many an imaginary dust-bath in my hair, followed by a gambol, rushing through it from one ear to the other and swinging on the curls.

There was a gradual improvement in the co-ordination of the wings as he grew, but it would have been madness to have put him out of doors so, as he seemed quite happy, I decided to let him live permanently in the house. The great moment of the day was in the early morning when I took the cover from his cage and let him climb—chattering with excitement—into my bed to share my tea and toast. He loved milk and drank quantities of it. There seems to be a milky way to the hearts of many wild birds, and I have known young starlings and blackbirds leave their mothers in the garden and follow me all round the house for a taste of this coveted beverage. My foundling, of course, having been brought up on it, was already a milk addict.

After breakfast, if the siren allowed, came the " Morning Scrap." The bed would be cleared for action and I would sit at one end and the sparrow, looking like a miniature eagle, at the other. Then he would rush at me, tail spread and wings outstretched, and hold down my hand with one tiny claw while he hammered it with his beak like a miner with a pickaxe. He would then retreat only to return in fury to the attack—pecking, pinching, tumbling and scolding as the wild sparrows do in the hedgerows. But when I said sternly, " Now, now ! That's enough ! " he would simmer down and flutter his fan until he was fed. Unfortunately he soon discovered that there were vulnerable points in my anatomy such as lobes of ears, quicks of finger-nails and, of course, eyes, and I had to protect myself by wearing goggles during these furious encounters, but he enjoyed them and they were good exercise for his wings.

It was a point of honour between us that there was to be no

fighting with me at any other time of the day and, though he attacked my visitors whenever they annoyed him, he never broke faith with me in this respect. There were no blots on his escutcheon. He seemed to understand much of what I said to him by the tone of my voice, but all attempts on my part to teach him to talk were unsuccessful. The nearest approach to articulation was a peculiar and very unbirdlike sound he often made when I covered him for the night — something like " um-m-m-m," plaintive and intimate, as if intended as a last loving salutation at the close of the day.

By this time I had added more variety to his menu, hemp-seed, lettuce, apple and sweet biscuits being first favourites. Canary-seed he ate readily if obtainable, and he enjoyed meat, fish (particularly Dover sole and Scotch salmon) and roast chicken—in fact almost anything except nuts, and he liked his Fifty-Seven Varieties. He objected strongly, however, to the flavour of onions, and if I offered him meat from an Irish Stew he would edge away without so much as a taste, a fact that raises a doubt in my mind as to the truth of the popular belief that birds (with the exception of geese) have no sense of smell. I used to tease him sometimes by offering him a titbit and then running away to hide in another part of the house. It was amusing to hear him hurrying from room to room in search of me, the rapid hop-hop-hop of his little feet sounding (even on the thick pile of the carpet) like a tiny machine-gun. When I called him I found he had answered before the words had left my lips, hearing I suppose the intake of the breath before articulation, and the game was won and the prize awarded almost before I had finished the sentence.

When left alone in the house he seemed quite content. I often watched through the window to satisfy my mind that he was not fretting in my absence, but apparently, as soon as he realised that I had gone, he settled down and amused himself with his food and toys. I had provided him with a great variety of playthings, but the only ones that ever appealed to him were hairpins, patience-cards and matches which he would carry about in his cage by the hour. Once he knew I was in the house, however, toys were discarded and I occupied his whole attention. He was a most persistent little person. He couldn't bear me out of his sight for one moment, and the sound of his voice and the patter of his little feet seemed to fill every room until I found it difficult to believe that I had not adopted a whole nestful of birds.

Yet, in spite of all his youthful energy and high spirits, he was ready at any hour of the day to share my slumbers. When I was confined to bed for a fortnight with a severe attack of the measles he lived in a state of bliss. Every day was field-day and life became " one constant round of pleasure." He shared my food, and cuddled under the bedclothes more or less all day, though occasionally he climbed back into his cage to attend to his toilet and to take a nibble between meals as children love to do, and then rushed back to me with a chirrup of joy. He fought, scolded and bullied the District Nurse and amused her so intensely that she brought her patients to see for themselves what they had refused to believe, with the result that he took on the whole crowd and fought them *en masse* until he had vanquished them all. One day a visitor brought in a young sparrow from the garden who seemed disposed to be friendly, but he attacked it at once with such vituperation and indeed such ferocity that we had to restore it to its anxious parents with all possible speed. He was very upset about this, and continued muttering and swearing under his breath until I conciliated him with an offering of hemp-seed. Snatching it from my fingers he retired with a great show of wounded dignity and hid himself behind my pillow. We never tried this experiment again and he remained my contented and devoted companion until I returned to work.

Few foundlings have risen to fame in human history, though there have been notable exceptions such as Romulus and Remus if legend can be believed. Moses, of course, was the greatest foundling the world has ever known, but even he was not deprived of a mother's love and care, and the life of a child who has never known the inestimable blessing of a good home is often a tragedy.

My sparrow, however, though an outcast, was to prove himself a Child of Destiny and to rise to a place of honour only accorded once before in the world's history to one of his race. This strange story is told in later chapters.

He was now nearly three months old—happy, healthy and full of confidence—and, though petted and spoiled by all who knew him, he remained lovable, tractable and, on the whole, obedient.

So happily passed his babyhood.

CHAPTER TWO

HIS LIFE AS AN ACTOR

The exigencies of war bring fame and recognition to many who would otherwise have remained in obscurity. Not only courage—which becomes so universal that we almost cease to notice it—but talents and even genius, hitherto latent and unsuspected, are brought to light in the most unexpected places and shine brightly against the dark background of tribulation. It is my belief that we all live on the very edge of inspiration ; that even the humblest of us are potential artists.

On his own level even my little sparrow rose to fame during the dark days of the blitz, for he became an actor and, though his career was a short one, he gave genuine pleasure to many of London's weary citizens while it lasted.

In September, as many of us remember only too well, the bombing began in earnest. Every time I left him and went on duty at the call of the siren I knew that I might never see him again. Towards the end of the month a delayed action bomb fell immediately behind my bungalow and, as I was forbidden to return and find him a place of greater safety, I watched my neighbour's house go up in smoke, and was resigned to the worst. As soon as I was released I flew home and, bursting into the room where I had left his cage, called out : " Are you alive ? " A little voice replied at once and, when the atmosphere had cleared, I saw him sitting placidly in his swing—apparently unhurt. It was a wonderful escape since he was practically the only thing undamaged in the house. The roof of his cage had been staved in, a brick lay upon it within an inch of his head, and the floor was thick with broken glass, but he was quite unperturbed. Was it chance or instinct, I wonder, that prompted him to take refuge in his swing in this emergency—thereby minimising the effect of blast ? Instinct I think it must have been for ever after, when the guns roared and the earth shook,

28

he immediately went into this retreat and stayed quietly swaying there until all was calm again. He never showed any fear at any time during the raids, although they annoyed him at night and he would ring his bell and rattle his bars if the noise was louder than usual.

As my bungalow had become temporarily uninhabitable, we moved to a more spacious home in the district which was vacant. This house had also suffered heavily from the attentions of the Luftwaffe and stood up, gaunt, battered, windowless, amid the greater desolation that surrounded it. It was watertight, however, and as the front door was still in its place, it afforded us some measure of security. We were joined there, soon after our arrival, by some refugees, relatives of my late husband. These people, to my great consternation, brought a cat, so my sparrow had to be confined to barracks and live in perpetual twilight in a small upstairs room. Thus life for me became more than usually anxious. There was a terrible moment one morning when I found the door of this room ajar and the cat sitting at the side of my sparrow's cage staring fixedly within. The sparrow was standing, quite motionless, on its floor in the corner nearest to his enemy, mercifully protected by the surrounding strip of glass which (so long as he remained behind it) made an effective barrier between them. I dare not credit him with sufficient intelligence to have chosen deliberately the only place of safety. It must have been a lucky chance, but after that the door was locked and the key removed.

It was a dreary life for the little fellow, though he seemed happy and made no complaints. We at least had the excitement of the bombs and, as the old lady said in the East End, " Those blooming air-raids did take your mind off the war," but there was nothing to amuse him.

Shortly afterwards I was sent on relief-duty to a hard-pressed Post in a poorer part of London where many of my colleagues were navvies and street-hawkers. It was a great experience and education for me. At first they resented my intrusion, but as time went on we became the best of friends and I remember them with affection and admiration. Their Cockney humour was delightful. A daily code-word for the Civil Defence was introduced while I was there and caused a great deal of amusement. I arrived one morning in time to hear a heated discussion on the possible meaning of the word " novice." No one seemed to have the least idea what it meant or how to pronounce it and, for fear of being considered an intellectual snob, I refrained from joining in. However, the appearance of Mr. S., the window cleaner, settled the matter. " Blimey ! " he said. " It means ' Pray for us ! ' (pronounced ' Pry.') Don't you know that old song my mother used to sing, Ora pro Novice ? " This explanation was accepted at once, the general opinion being that, as we had already had twelve serious incidents in the sector within the last two days, the word was very appropriate. He was a charming man, this window cleaner, the life and soul of the party, and we missed him terribly when he left to join what he called the " Damconteminition Squad." The courage and steadfastness of all the men was beyond praise, but the boredom from which they suffered when there was a lull in the enemy's activities was so demoralising that I racked my brains to think of something to amuse them and, quite by chance, discovered that Natural History interested them more than any other subject.

It was then that I had an inspiration. Why not teach the sparrow to entertain us in our dull moments ? I took him in hand at once and, as he raised no objection, I taught him some little tricks with the help of his favourite toys. He learned with extraordinary ease and rapidity, and I began to take him with me to various Posts, to houses where there were nervous people and, more often, to a Rest Centre where he had a great reception particularly from children. To them he was a never-failing delight. I can say with complete truth that no sparrow ever served his country so faithfully and so efficiently as he did in those terrible months. People who had lost their homes and all their possessions forgot their troubles, at least for the time being ; terrified children became merry and carefree, and those who had obstinately refused to allow their gas-masks to be fitted held up their heads at once if promised a game with the sparrow. Indeed he became quite an important member of the Civil

Defence, doing useful and valiant work as an entertainer when the blitz was at its height, and he very seldom disappointed an audience. Even at houses where people were hostile and where I had been sullenly refused admittance, the doors were often opened with a smile and a cheery word if the young actor accompanied me. Little stories about him, and greeting-cards with a sketch on the cover, were bought eagerly in aid of the Red Cross and found their way into homes and hospitals, not only in England but overseas in the more remote corners of the earth.

He began his performance by sitting sedately in his historic pudding-basin, where he was fed with hemp-seeds by favoured ticket-holders from the front row of the stalls. Then, as gay and light of foot as a ballet-dancer, he would leap out and, suddenly transforming himself into an Infant Hercules with set brows and straining muscles, he would engage me in a tug-of-war with a hairpin, holding it tenaciously in his beak, pulling with all his might until I allowed him to win and carry his trophy in triumph to his cage. After a curtain and a brief interval he would re-appear in the role of conjuror and pick a card from a hand presented to him, usually the one chosen by the audience if I pointed to it or pushed it very slightly forward. When he tired of this he took a patience-card in his beak, and turned it round ten or twelve times without dropping it as he rounded the corners. This, I believe, was his favourite trick, for it was self-taught and he amused himself with it for years after he had left the footlights and had forgotten all the others.

Matches also were a favourite toy and he would take one from a box and run it backwards and forwards through his beak, to the accompaniment of a small musical box, as if playing the flute. If presented with a half-burnt match he seized it eagerly and devoured the blackened end with evident enjoyment, which made me wonder if the wild birds eat charcoal from our bonfires as an aid to digestion. Sometimes, during the interval for refreshment, he took an imaginary bath in the front page of the *Times*. Apparently he mistook the printed letters for dust or insects, and on one occasion tried to pick them up, one by one, and put them under his wings—an action which looked to me suspiciously like "anting," but unfortunately there were no ornithologists present to confirm my suspicions. He usually worked in silence, for I do not think he possessed a sense of humour, but an occasional chirrup, which the audience took for a quip or an epigram, brought a ripple of laughter from the pit. His most popular number, however, was his famous " Air-Raid-Shelter Trick " which never failed to bring down the house and gave him many curtains. I had taught him to sit down in my left hand—at first by putting hemp-seeds there—while I cupped it with my right. Thereafter it was comparatively easy to associate this action with the repetition of certain words and before long I had only to say : " Siren's gone ! " and he would run into this improvised shelter, sit quite motionless for several minutes and then poke out his head as if enquiring if the All-Clear had yet sounded.

This spectacular performance was a great source of joy to all the younger members of the audience, and they would queue up for the privilege of sheltering him in their own hands. The person who gave *me* the most pleasure, however, was a somewhat pompous old lady who remarked as she looked at him through her lorgnettes, " Dear me ! What a wonderful little creature ! He shows remarkable intelligence for a cold-blooded animal ! " (The normal temperature of a sparrow I understand is 110 degrees).

So the weeks flew by, and the actor, if he wasn't showered with bouquets, was presented by his numerous fans with many tributes more suited to his taste. In fact he was wined and dined so frequently that he put on weight and was in danger of becoming lazy and self-indulgent. I am sure that, when I myself am dead and forgotten, there will be many people who will tell their children and grandchildren about the sparrow who entertained them in London during the Blitz. By a curious coincidence only a few weeks ago (I am writing this in the year 1952) a friend of mine on holiday in Sussex overheard a lady recounting to some children, who were listening spellbound, the story of my bird's performance at a Rest Centre.

Of course there were frequent interruptions, when the theatre

Fancy being brought up in this! But many famous men had humble beginnings

I can turn this round ten times without dropping it. It's not easy. Try it!

Choose your own card and I'll pick it out

The Air-Raid-Shelter-Trick. Has the All-clear gone yet?

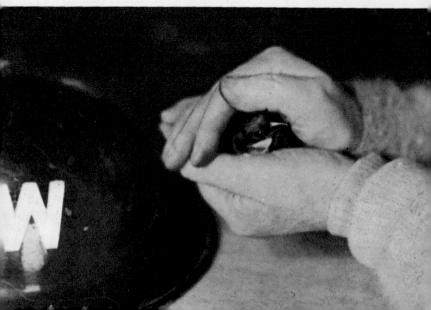

had to close down abruptly and the star performer was hustled unceremoniously into his cage.

The question of a name for the sparrow arose about this time, so the matter was discussed at the next Warden's Meeting. An actor of his ability must have a name if only to blazon on his posters ! My original intention had been to christen him " Clarissa," for, on account of his pale grey chest and the absence of male markings, I had mistaken him for a hen ; but after his first moult he suddenly appeared with an Old School Tie, that patch of black or very dark brown under the chin which is the Sparrow's Badge of Manhood. So feminine an appellation, therefore, had become an insult. " Let's call him Clarence ! said the children, and, preposterous as it may seem, Clarence he became, though he never owned it, answering only to the name of " Boy."

I never took him out with me when the Bomber's Moon was high in the sky or when the raids were likely to be heavy, but on one occasion we were caught out together in the Blitz and the black-out, and had an adventurous experience that might well have caused his death and cut short a life of great promise. On my way home from a children's party where he had surpassed himself, I was asked by a young soldier if I could direct him to a small and somewhat isolated station about a mile from my home ; he had to report at a new camp that had just been opened in its vicinity. Both station and camp were familiar to me and, as the young man was a stranger in the district, I offered to take him to his camp gates. I was retracing my steps when my torch went out and, in a darkness that was almost solid, I lost my way. Fortunately my little actor was in a small felt-lined box with a perforated lid which we sometimes used as a travelling-carriage, and I had the good sense to button this securely into the breast of my Warden's tunic.

The once-familiar station was so severely damaged that it was unrecognisable, and the ground was as full of craters as the surface of the moon. Weary with wandering and stumbling over debris I sat down to collect my thoughts and try to recover my bearings and found, to my horror, that I was leaning against

C

a train. Whether this was standing in a siding or on the Permanent Way it was impossible to tell. It was a night, not of stars but of almost Stygian blackness lit faintly at intervals by the luminous groping fingers of distant searchlights. During a lull in the bombardment when the drone of hostile wings had temporarily died away I called repeatedly for help, but there was no reply. Fearful lest the train should suddenly begin to move I jumped up, ran forward a few paces and fell headlong into a deep and slippery crater. Down and down we went—the sparrow and I—until my feet, encased in their heavy gumboots, sank into the slime and water at the bottom. By great good fortune this welter was not deep enough to reach above my knees, and, as all my frantic efforts to scale the reeking sides of the pit were unavailing, I resigned myself to my fate and waited patiently for the dawn.

Presently I heard the All-Clear sound and the little bird stirred in his box. Then all was still again. It was a long night, but Londoners had grown accustomed to interminable hours of danger and discomfort and my companion at least was warm and dry. Day broke at last, and eventually I found a way of escape. I crawled home, covered with mud and half-frozen. This, except for the bombing of the bungalow, was the sparrow's biggest adventure of the war. He probably slept blissfully through most of it but I took care never to be out in the dark with him again.

Unhappily in the Spring of 1941 he began to tire of public life and all its glamour, and became unaccountably shy and unwilling to entertain. He also developed a nasty little habit of pinching people's hands, so, as his popularity was on the wane, his visits to Post and Rest Centre were discontinued. I thought it best for him to retire gracefully—as all great artists are well-advised to do—while at the height of his powers. Henceforth he lived exclusively *chez moi* and devoted himself to me as his only-desired companion.

No doubt he could have been trained to professional life and might have become very famous. On Television, if the little streaked and speckled egg out of which he must have emerged before I met him had been laid a few years later, he might have been a first favourite. I do not think he would have enjoyed full-time professional work, however, and I do not approve of the continued exploitation of animals for human entertainment, when it is evidently at variance with their nature and inclination. It is true that my sparrow was a performing bird, but only in a private and exclusive Dramatic Society. His little tricks, though they showed undoubted intelligence and adaptability, were in reality only the development of his natural instincts. They were just things he liked doing, and I never persuaded him to learn anything against his will.

From babyhood he had shared, " so far as his irrational nature allowed," my moods and my indoor activities. When I cooked he watched me and tasted anything he enjoyed from a spoon ; when I played he sat on my hand and listened ; when I read he settled down on my wrist and often looked at the words to which I pointed, and when I slept he shared my slumbers. But he was always free to leave me if he wished and find his own form of amusement. In this way I kept his confidence, and his training, if such it can be called, was so gradual and so integral a part of our growing companionship that it became the expression of his own nature.

After his first moult he was really a beautiful little bird. Much daintier, more graceful in his movements, sleeker and more streamlined than his male relatives in garden and gutter, he also displayed a good deal more colour. In addition to a decidedly yellowish collar, he sported a saffron waistcoat and primrose pants. This unusual brilliance of plumage was probably due to colour-feeding with yolk of egg since, after this useful article of food became almost obsolete and the mere mention of it an anachronism, it faded very noticeably. His beak and toe-nails were like polished ebony, and even the " fan-wing " was decorative and certainly distinctive.

How fortuitously heredity and environment had connived together in the creation of this little bird, already so distinct from others of his species. Of these two great influences environment, so far, had proved the stronger.

CHAPTER THREE

HIS LIFE OF MUSIC

Two thousand years ago Catullus wrote of his famous sparrow who could " both dance and sing " in a poem translated into English by John Skelton (1460-1529). Since then countless myriads of these birds have chirped and twittered down the centuries, and it may seem incredible to many people that they could be taught to sing : but I am speaking the truth when I say that my Sparrow took up music as a profession at a very early age and learned to express himself in trill and cadence.

I cannot remember precisely when he began to sing, as I was not the first person privileged to hear him ; but it must have been sometime in January 1941, when he was only six months old. I was already aware of the fact that, although many of the sounds he uttered were the common language of sparrows, many of them were not. The range and variety of his notes and calls were remarkable, and he was continually adding to them until— as a mere stripling—he must have wielded (like Mr. Winston Churchill on a higher intellectual level) the most formidable vocabulary of his generation. His famous " Hitler Speeches," as the children called them, which he had delivered for our edification—his fan-wing lifted high as if in Nazi salute—ever since he was out of his cradle, had increased in length until they lasted, with only a few short breaks, for nearly three minutes and a half. It is true they bore some resemblance to the chattering of sparrows in the hedgerows ; yet they were distinctly different and rose, like oratory, from a solemn and impressive statement, by gradual crescendos, to a fiery and impassioned climax. But these perorations gave me no reason to suspect that the little master of rhetoric possessed any latent musical talent.

Ever since he was out of, or rather into, his petticoats, and whenever I was off duty in the early morning, I had put him on my shoulder and, carrying him to the grand piano, had played to him for over an hour. He showed, almost from the first day, that he was affected and excited by the music. Not only his wing but his whole body would quiver, and he would pinch my neck, twisting little bits of the flesh until my scales became suddenly staccato, as if his emotions were too strong for him. Whether this was an expression on his part of pleasure or pain I cannot say : it may have been both, but I never dreamed for one moment that he would learn to sing.

My surprise can well be imagined when my refugees informed me one day that my foundling had been singing in the twilight-solitude of his room upstairs, and practising turns and little trills. I thought they must be mistaken and had heard a bird outside, so nothing more was said about it for several weeks. Suddenly, one morning as I was running water from the bath-room tap, I heard it myself—a strange little song—clearly and unmistakably coming from the locked room. It began with twitterings ; then there was a little turn, an attempt at melodic outline, a high note (far above the vocal register of a sparrow) and then—wonder of wonders !—a little trill. I listened spell-bound at the door, and he went on practising assiduously ; but when I entered the room he stopped at once and fluttered his fan. A few days later I heard him again, and as Spring advanced his hours of practice increased until, by the end of the Summer, he seemed to be singing every day.

Of course, being still a student, he naturally refused to accept any engagements. That would be letting the profession down. So many visitors, foolishly invited to hear him before he was ready, went away believing me to be the victim of hallucination. However, like a true nympholept, he always fell under the spell of running water, and I found, in the course of time, that the sound of it usually provided the required stimulus for a musical outburst. In the early Autumn, to my great joy, he added another little trill to his score, and his song became a finished and highly creditable performance.

At the end of the year my refugees and their cat returned to Folkestone—the scare of bombardment having temporarily died down—and once again my little bird and I had a house to ourselves. I began the music-lessons again, playing to him whenever there was an opportunity, and my joy was great when he began to follow me to the piano of his own accord, climb on to my shoulder and sing to my accompaniment.

One day in early Spring, as by this time the young musician could usually be relied upon to honour his engagements, I arranged a little informal concert so that he could make his debut as an operatic tenor. Six or seven people accepted the invitation and, after tea, the stage was set for the First Appearance of the Infant Prodigy. The audience was seated, breathless and expectant, at some distance from the piano, and the doors, both of the music-room and of an apartment opposite which served as the Artist's Room, were opened wide. I took my seat at the keyboard, and all eyes were focused on the floor at the threshold.

For several minutes after I began to play nothing happened. There was neither sight nor sound of the artist, and my heart sank. Then someone said in a stage-whisper, "Hush ! He's coming ! " and a moment later a minute figure appeared in the doorway. I cannot truthfully say that his entrance was a success. It was not impressive and it lacked style. Perhaps he felt some tenseness in the atmosphere that he did not understand. However, after stopping on the hearthrug to arrange his coat-tails or, to be more exact, to draw the feathers of his tail one by one through his beak, he half ran and half flew across the room—as if the cat were after him—and scrambled up my leg and on to my shoulder. The silence could be felt. Once again there was an anti-climax and it looked as if the money for the tickets would have to be returned, for he sat there for several minutes, quietly preening his feathers.

At long last, after more rapid trilling and rippling from me in the upper register of the piano, he began to tune up and suddenly burst into full song to the accompaniment of the Black Study. This, alas ! was his swan-song as a Concert Artist, for the applause so terrified him that he disappeared down my neck and never sang in public again.

Nevertheless, our own private and intimate recitals continued to be a joy to me for several years. He loved music that trilled, and scales played rapidly in the treble; and, though I do not for a moment suggest that he knew one piece from another, some undoubtedly had a special appeal and inspired him to more spontaneous outbursts. I always think that he learned to trill from Chopin's Berceuse, but that of course is impossible to prove. He never sang so well as in the early morning and, as I played faster and faster, and higher and higher in the treble, he would pour out his soul in an ecstacy as great, if not as melodious, as any skylark.

I very much regret that I was unable to obtain a record of my sparrow's song when it was at its best, for it would surely have been unique and might well have been accorded an honoured place in the Library of the Songs of British Birds; but the incomparable Ludwig Koch was then unknown to us in England, recording was impossible at the time, and when the war was over and we had returned to more normal conditions, his performance had seriously deteriorated.

The song itself was in two sections—quite distinct from each other and sometimes sung separately. Indeed, people who listened to it from an adjoining room often remarked that more than one bird was singing. The first part, or introduction, was an expression of pleasure, good humour and simple *joie de vivre*, but the second—the *real* song—was an outpouring of rapture. Both parts were usually in the key of F Major although, unless my ear was at fault, the second part (when sung alone) varied in pitch by as much as a minor third, according to its intensity.

The introduction began with the usual sparrow-chirpings, though less harsh in tone than those that sometimes weary us with their monotony in the early morning, and descended by a perfect fourth from tonic to dominant. (There is a sparrow chirping in fourths, from F down to C, outside my window at the moment). This interval was followed by a perfect fifth descending from G to C; and these two were repeated and ornamented with mordents or (sometimes) with four-note trills. Then followed a rapid triplet leading back to the tonic and repeated indefinitely. I wrote it down, and give it here :—

I grieve to say that I never transcribed the second half of the song, which was by far the more musical of the two ; and as my small virtuoso has not even practised since his illness, and I have not heard it for many months, I cannot do so now with any confidence as to its accuracy. All I can say is that it opened with an eight-note trill, followed by a high, sweet, plaintive note. Then, descending by an interval of which I am not quite sure, it rose again to a second trill of eight notes a perfect fourth higher than the first. This theme was repeated several times and sometimes ended abruptly but more often returned to the tonic. The tone lacked the clarity of our best songsters, but there was undoubted beauty in the high notes. Except in the preliminary tuning-up, the song was distinctive and, so far as I know, unlike that of any other bird. If the cage stood in the window it could be heard some distance down the road and recognised at once. There was no rubato, only an increase in intensity that gave the impression of acceleration in moments of supreme joy. Except during the first week of the moult he sang all the year round and often treated us to a carol on Christmas Day.

Only once in my hearing did either of the trills exceed eight notes, which was a great disappointment to me. At the end of his fifth year I am sorry to say he discarded the higher and more musical of these embellishments, substituting a harsh croaking noise that sounded as if he were clearing his throat, but of which he seemed inordinately proud. His artistry was not impeccable, but sparrows are not a musical family, and his performance at its best was an achievement for one of his species.

All attempts on my part to stimulate his ambition and rouse him to greater efforts were unsuccessful. I tried him with a record of Beatrice Harrison's Nightingale, but he was not interested and preferred the vacuum cleaner or the typewriter. To the British Broadcasting Corporation he was indifferent, except that it annoyed him after he had retired to bed, when he rang his bell and rattled his bars until the radio was turned down.

I provided him with a mirror hoping he would sing to it as canaries do but even that failed to interest him. Instead, he became intrigued with the heavy brass bell that hung from his roof and began to wriggle it off its hook and carry it about. Sometimes he held this by the rim and sometimes by the clapper when it so completely obscured his vision that he often fell head over heels and had to abandon it. It is quite possible that this Herculean feat of strength was intended to impress his rival in the glass, for when I removed the mirror the bell remained on its hook.

As a last hope I borrowed a Hartz Mountain Roller Canary and hid it behind a screen quite close to his cage so that he could hear it singing hour after hour ; but, except that he ceased to sing until it left off, he took no notice of it. I never heard him make the slightest attempt to imitate or to emulate it, though the canary was stimulated to supreme efforts of coloratura virtuosity and very soon shouted him down. At the end of a week, as the experiment was a failure, I returned the visitor to its owner and my bird resumed his usual practice as if it had never been interrupted. No doubt my experiment was made too late in life. He had learned his song at the piano during his first year and, though he improved its tone and fluency by constant work, except for the deterioration that I have already mentioned, he never varied its notation but only its pitch. He was concerned solely with the development of his own peculiar talent, and I am sure no bird ever worked harder to bring his song to per-fection. He practised constantly, repeating each little motif over and over again, and biting the bars of his cage in a perfect agony of self-expression. Of such stuff are all true artistes made ! Suffering is the only college in which they can gain degrees.

Would my sparrow have sung if I had not been at one time a professional musician and still endeavoured to keep up my practice ? That is a question I often asked myself. Was I Svengali and he my Trilby ? I cannot tell. All I know assuredly is that intelligence is latent in all animals and birds, and can be developed in varying degrees according to the measure of love and companionship bestowed upon them by man. Literature is full of amazing stories that are in themselves proof of this statement, the most touching that I have ever read being that of the famous " Tramp-Dog of Quebec " who, having seen his master's departure by sea, met vessels arriving at the Quay for five years and, refusing all offers of shelter and affection, died apparently of a broken heart.

Buffalo Bill's horse, when his master fell from his back and hung perilously on the ledge of a precipice, galloped home for assistance, whinnying and pawing the ground until someone rode him back to the scene of the tragedy and rescued his master. Later, when his master died, he nosed the dead face in the coffin with every manifestation of grief. I will only add one story of my own for the truth of which I can vouch.

A missionary doctor in Singapore at the time of the fall of that city was in charge of a First Aid Post when a small mongrel dog was brought in with an injured leg. It was successfully treated and sent home a few days later. The following week she and the nurses noticed a dog approaching the tent dragging some cumbersome object. It was her former patient. He had brought a hassock which he must have stolen from the Cathedral, and laying it at the doctor's feet as a gift of gratitude, with a joyous bark and much wagging of the tail, he disappeared.

I have been told that the most untrustworthy and untameable of all beasts is the British bull, and yet in my childhood I knew of a white bull, unringed and completely tractable, which was ridden regularly into the village where I was born by the farmer who had bred it. It was guided only by his voice and a rope attached to a noseband, and it could be trusted to wait for him patiently outside a shop or a public house.

I have seen a huge hippopotamus lift its great squelching mouth from a pool at the Zoo in answer to the name of " Daisy " when its keeper called, and come to him like a dog. Still lower in the scale of animal intelligence I have known hedgehogs, toads and even slow-worms that recognised their owners and showed some sign of recognition at their approach. Birds are surely more intelligent than the lowest of these creatures and as yet, as ornithologists agree, we know very little about them.

Just as a puppy learns to copy his master and acquires some of his characteristics and even a measure of his personality, my sparrow copied me unconsciously in many ways. I will give but one example. Whenever I receive a letter, parcel or other communication that I have reason to believe will afford me great pleasure, I like to delay opening it until I have made myself as tidy and presentable as if I were expecting a guest and arranged myself where I can enjoy that pleasure in comfort and with some degree of dignity. It is just one of those queer idiosyncrasies that develop in the characters of people who live alone. In much the same way, when my small bird knew that he might expect some particularly toothsome morsel of food or a spoonful of cream and sugar, he often prepared for it by preening his feathers and settling himself in some specially-chosen place before he accepted the gift. This happened often enough in all the years before his illness to be called a habit and it cannot be dismissed as a coincidence.

I do not approve of a slavish devotion to animals, though I infinitely prefer it to cruelty, or a slavish devotion to self. I agree that " animals should be kept in their place," but has not man, to a great extent, forgotten what that place should be, and has he not, on the whole, betrayed his trust to the so-called brute-creation ? Thank God the last hundred years has seen an awakening in some countries of the public conscience and the rise of many societies for the protection of animals and birds. And yet in England to-day we still find that abomination of wickedness, the steel-toothed gin-trap. When fear has once been cast out, an animal becomes responsive to affection and the results, as we know, are often astonishing. My sparrow sang because I played and because he knew I loved him. That, I believe, is the answer to the question I have just postulated.

I would give much to possess a photograph of him at that time with his fan-wing fluttering in sympathy with the throbbing of his little throat, but the opportunity was unfortunately lost for ever. Actually the distorted wing grew a little less upright after each moult until, at the age of eleven, it was hardly noticeable. This, I think, was a pity, for it marked him out from other birds, and if one has enough courage and force of personality, a deformity can become a distinction. By the time he was four years old he could fly across the room, uncertainly but with increasing confidence.

As may easily be imagined, the young musician soon began to attract the attention of the wild birds of the neighbourhood. I used to hide in the bushes and watch them fly to his window, sometimes singly, sometimes in twos and threes, and stand there staring and jostling each other in obvious astonishment. If birds are addicted to gossip, there must have been a good deal of it going on in the bushes and on the roof-tops over the strange relative with a crooked wing who lived in a house he couldn't get out of and sang quite differently from anybody else! Sparrows, tits and an occasional robin appeared to be the most interested and I only wish I were sufficiently conversant with bird-language to have translated their remarks.

Yet my sparrow, like all our songsters, loved his quiet hours, and especially his noonday rest. It was no small part of our perfect companionship that we could enjoy long hours of peaceful contemplation together. I am not a lover of noise, nor yet of too much melody. I like a background of silence on which to hang my thoughts. Then if they are unworthy I can replace them by others that are greater than my own. Music can thrill, console, inspire and deepen the very roots of life, but it is in the silence that man's spirit grows.

It would have been interesting to know if my sparrow had been successfully mated, whether any of his off-spring, brought up in similar circumstances, would have sung, and perhaps reached a higher musical standard. Since he remained a celibate all his life, that is a question to which there can be no answer.

With regard to his voice, his physical appearance, beauty of plumage, and intelligence, I think he reached his highest level in his fifth and sixth years. Possibly this is the prime of the

44

wild sparrow's life, if it is fortunate enough to reach it amid the rigours and jeopardies of outdoor life.

One of the most enchanting of all his musical moments to me was his burst of song, his Aubade at Dawn, as he flew to me for the day's first greeting. That will always be a treasured and ineffaceable memory.

CHAPTER FOUR

HIS LIFE OF LOVE

No biography is complete without a love story. At any rate, judging by the unwearied and quite immoral efforts of biographers to unearth the private letters of the Illustrious Dead in search of one, that would appear to be the popular opinion.

But my sparrow's love-affairs—if he had any—were shadowy, nebulous and immature. If Cupid's darts ever struck his little heart they must have glanced off and left no scars.

I wonder sometimes if it would have been kinder and wiser never to have allowed him to see the birds outside. He would have probably remained to the end of his life a grown-up nestling, and perhaps a more completely contented companion for me. But light and fresh air were very beneficial to his health, and, on the whole, I felt that, if he were ever dimly conscious of privation and frustration when he looked out upon the world of nature that he might never enter, he was compensated for it by a more clearly-defined sense that he was loved and of great importance.

For the first four years of his life, though he had often perched or played on the window-ledge, he had never shown the slightest interest in anything that lay beyond it. I was his little world, and the only time I had taken him into the garden he had hidden himself in my dress ; but when I began to stand his cage in the window he gradually became aware of the wild life that chirped and fluttered ever nearer to him.

It was interesting to watch this gradual awakening, but the new intimacy with the wild birds changed him in many ways. By some mysterious means, only partially explained by their example, they taught him fear. The sight of a cat—which he had previously regarded with indifference—threw him into a panic, and I had to fasten a gauze curtain across the lower pane of his window so that, though he could see the trees and sky,

46

any creature on the ground would be invisible to him. Then he began to show uneasiness if anything passed or hung above his head; and if I held my hand over him, as if hovering like a hawk, he would look up at it, with his feathers flattened, and crouch as if afraid. But the window cleaner was the principal actor in his Grand Guignol. Quite possibly the man's hand, with its queer circling and pouncing movements, suggested the paw of an immense predatory animal, but, whatever the reason, the terror it inspired was so unmistakable that I had to move his cage and cover it with a dark cloth.

There were times when my heart smote me as I watched him fly to the fanlight (for he could manage a short flight by that time) in answer to the calls of his companions, piping to them himself with a high, thin, piercing note; and yet, when they came into the room as they began to do quite fearlessly before many weeks had passed, he seemed utterly indifferent to them. He would look up at me, with an absurdly self-conscious expression, as if to say : " Am I expected to know these people ? " and he seemed relieved when they were gone. The only time he ever showed any desire to join in their activities was when they were fighting in little groups, tumbling and scolding in the bushes, for he dearly loved a scrap and felt no doubt that he could have shown them a thing or two. He never displayed to them, to my knowledge, or took the faintest interest in the tits and sparrows that, quite obviously, threw themselves (metaphorically) at his feet.

Married women, or perhaps it would be safer to say women of marriageable age, visited him continually in the Spring and Summer and declared their love openly and without shame. A robin was a constant visitor, and sparrows, accompanied by their men-folk who pecked and admonished them at intervals, sat on the edge of my bed until I drove them away for the sake of cleanliness. These last, of course, may have been trippers who had flocked in through idle curiosity.

The most moonstruck of his presumably female admirers was a little blue-tit. She haunted his window from dawn to dusk, fluttering up and down, pecking at it and pleading piteously to be admitted to the object of her tender passion. When I opened the fanlight she flew straight in and, utterly regardless either of my proximity or my interference, hovered at the side of his cage or perched on the roof quivering her wings in the most unmaidenly manner. Manlike, for men hate a scene and have a very wise aversion to hysterical women, he ignored her utterly. He usually descended to his kitchen and made a great show of cracking seeds until I removed her with my hand and relieved him from his embarrassment.

She courted him for three successive seasons, but her youthful beauty and all her dainty feminine wiles availed her nothing. The sparrow's heart remained adamant, and if any tears of unrequited love were shed in the tender dusk of a summer's evening, they must have fallen on the far side of the window-pane. What became of her I never knew. Perhaps like Elaine, the Lily-Maid, she died for love of her Launcelot, and there being no bright barge and no shining river in the tiny rose-garden of a suburban bungalow, the Burying-Beetles bore her unsung and unlamented to an early grave. To him it must all have passed like a play in which he had no part. I think he was puzzled throughout his life by birds and never fully understood their relationship to himself. Then I had only to call him from my bed, or even from the door, to bring him flying to nestle at my neck forgetful of all else.

But he made love *to me* from March to October, strutting up and down on my hand and arm, spreading his wings and tail, looking up at me, with crest erect, bowing continually and going through all the familiar antics of courtship : and if I went near my bed, even to lay something down, when he was in his cage, he would dash round and round, pecking at the door in his anxiety to join me there and start housekeeping without further delay.

I fancy the afternoon siesta under the eiderdown began to acquire a new significance at this time, and changed in his little mind from the nest of his babyhood to the nest that he had made for himself. Not infrequently he would take a matchstick, or preferably a hairpin, into the retreat, approaching cautiously as if in fear of being seen or followed ; and though these treasures,

The Music Lesson

Accompanists are always late

I think I'll help with the proof-reading and see what she's been saying about me!

Where's she gone, I wonder!

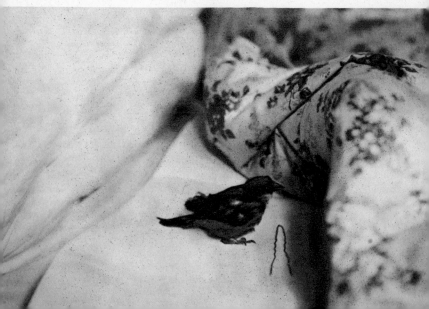

probably intended for foundation-stones, were always lost or discarded before he had finally settled on his nesting-site, he would wriggle his small body in the place of his choice, pecking, pinching and pulling at the bedclothes and fussing with his beak until he had made it more rounded and comfortable. I had to close my eyes as he ran over my face en route with his hairpin, and was usually pecked, if he happened to drop it, as if he thought the fault were mine.

It is perhaps a little surprising that as a wild bird, at least by birth and inheritance, he never made any attempt at serious nest-building. He might have done so, of course, had he been mated, but that is something we shall never know. I often presented him with dried grass, moss, feathers, straw and other materials that can be purchased without price from Nature in her capacity of Builder's Merchant, but he either ignored them or ran away as if offended. I even offered him a primrose, knowing the fatal attraction of these flowers for his cousins in the garden, but he left it contemptuously on the edge of the bed. The flower " a yellow primrose was to him and it was nothing more," so he went back to his hairpins.

He would collect these from my hair—believing no doubt that they were put there for his use—run them into the bed, and then discard them as if they were not needed after all. Perhaps he felt that my Slumberland interior-sprung mattress, with its luxurious coverings, was sufficiently soft and warm to protect whatever nests were intended to contain. Of course, I had to be in my place to keep him company for, directly I left him, he either waited for me or returned to his cage, but so long as I was at his side he was more than satisfied, and shared his joy and pride of possession unquestioningly with me. Sometimes, if I moved or fidgeted, he would make queer little grumbling noises, very like a farmyard hen when she is disturbed on her eggs ; but, when all was quiet, he would murmur soft and incredibly happy little love-notes to himself (or to me) that would have been inaudible to anyone a few yards away. And often he would steal out of his secret nest, stand still a moment, and as he ran in again, burst into a sudden snatch of ecstatic song, the like

49

D

of which I have never heard surpassed for sheer rapture.

I am not one of " those whom the wild birds love." They do not fly to me unbidden as they flew to Saint Francis or to Henry David Thoreau ; and yet I wonder sometimes if any human being has ever communed with Nature—at least at this one focal point—more intimately than I have done, or gained so revealing a knowledge of the ecstacy that fills the hearts of little birds as they brood their eggs in secret places. I wonder, too, if more people were aware of the intensity of their happiness, whether there would be fewer ravaged and ruined nests in the countryside.

I began to indulge my sparrow in the enjoyment of his nest-fantasy more regularly in the Spring and Summer months. Although the war was approaching its final stage, I was still continually on night-duty and had earned a noonday rest. To ease my conscience, however, and save the waste of precious hours, I used to memorize page after page of music under the bedcover while he dreamed and brooded. When compelled to be busy in the house, I encouraged him to make a temporary nest just inside my jumper, and there he would sit by the hour, wrapt in his own happy dreams, or reminding me with small, sharp, ebony beak how often I disturbed them. Even this emergency nest he would keep scrupulously clean, flying back to his cage, whenever necessary, if it were in sight (otherwise anything handy would do !) for a wash and brush up, and returning to it again.

There were several other curious developments in his behaviour about this time that are worth recording. He learnt, I suppose from his wild visitors, to catch flies on the window-panes. This was remarkable, as he had always been indifferent to them, and had never tasted insect-food in his life. He hunted them with great skill, seized them ferociously and devoured them instantly with great relish.

He also took a sudden dislike to being caught, or rather taken hold of, or even to perching on my hand ; and made it quite clear that in future, when he came to me, he must be allowed to do so of his own accord. Instead of picking him up, or presenting him with my finger, I had to learn a new approach, and offer him my arm (and the right arm at that !) on to which he would hop with great dignity. Never once, until after his illness, did he relax his determination to insist on this as a point of etiquette. Occasionally he still consented to show off his parlour-tricks to a favoured visitor, but only if allowed to choose his own time and method of performance, and he would punish me with a vicious peck if I asked him for an encore.

In fact he had grown up. He had become a man and, except in rare moments of intimacy, he must show me that he was master and that I must do as I was told. Above all, I must give up moving furniture and other familiar landmarks from their accustomed places. He resented any change in his surroundings, and when the gardener cut down a tree outside his window he became almost demented ! Of course it was an important tree, having served as a grandstand for his female admirers, and like most men, though he refused the love of a lady, he still liked to be admired by her. It was several days before he became reconciled to his loss or, more probably, had forgotten it. He also strongly objected to my appearing in a new dress, and even a strange hat or a new pair of gloves called for loud protests. Once when I offered him a hemp-seed with a bandaged finger he flew away and refused to know me.

Then the cleaning of his cage, which had always annoyed him, became intolerable. He would hide, muttering in unprintable language, in the curtains or behind a cushion, poking out his head at intervals to see how the work was progressing ; and if, when he returned to it, the perches, food-dishes and bath were not in exactly the same place as when he left them, he would refuse to enter. I fancy this fastidiousness also had its roots in the nesting-instinct. Birds must be very observant to find their way back unerringly to their nests, and a broken bough, the altered position of a stone, or even a bent twig, may suggest an enemy. I can find no other reason for his behaviour, and it is probably the right one.

People often ask me why I did not present him with a hen-canary as a possible bride. My reason for refusing to do so was three-fold. First because quite obviously the nest (and nestlings) would have to be in my bed where I should have been expected to remain motionless quite indefinitely. Secondly, what should I do with my house full of little birds ? I hated the idea of selling his children, and their life in the open air would have been perilous in the extreme. Thirdly, I strongly suspected that, if he consented to marry, sooner or later he would have killed his wife in a fit of jealousy. So the experiment was never made.

On the three separate occasions when fledgling sparrows were brought to me from a cat's mouth, and I cared for each one until it died or was set free, he showed a sullen resentment both towards myself and the intruders. No doubt it would have been fairer to him if I had kept them in a separate room, but it was he who gave them confidence. I had only to settle a hungry mite comfortably in my hand, and when it had seen him fed through the bars of his cage it would take courage and begin to imitate. Soon they would be drinking fearlessly together from the same teaspoon, though I had to watch carefully or there would have been a vicious thrust from a jealous beak, and I never dared to leave them alone together.

They were all different, these little waifs. The first one adored me, and I had the greatest difficulty in persuading it to fly away. It came back again and again, and eventually I had to take it to a neighbour to set free. The second one, which was badly injured, climbed pathetically out of a little box into my hand to die there ; but the third had no use for me at all. Clarence was its idol, its hero, and it would stand for hours in front of his cage gazing up at him. When he chirped, fed, or preened his feathers it did the same. It was amusing to watch this slavish imitation ; yet, when taken into the garden, it flew away at once and never returned.

I had long been aware of the individuality of birds, which is the subject of Miss Len Howard's interesting book, " Birds as Individuals," and believed that there were outstanding person-alities to be found in every species, originals, pioneers, and perhaps even, on their own level, possessors of something very like genius. There may have been a single seagull that first discovered the green uplands as grand feeding grounds in time of storm, and perhaps a migrant that first led a flock across the ocean. All their activities must have had a beginning that was not entirely due to chance. It is a common platitude that no two living creatures are alike. Mass-production was never God's method of creation, and when we made it ours, however inevitable it may seem to us in the development of modern civilization, I believe we had travelled so far from His leading and direction that we took a sharp turn on to the road that led inevitably to disaster. We may yet have to retrace our steps.

Some years ago I looked after five pairs of canaries and one odd one for a lady who bred them, and of these eleven birds three were outstanding. One yellow cock and hen, whom I called Abelard and Heloise on account of their devotion, had always mated with each other, refusing all rivals. The little hen had never had a chick of her own, though she once laid an egg and was so excited that she put her foot through it. She made nest after nest and sat on each of them in succession, cuddling imaginary nestlings until her breast was nearly bare. One day I had an inspiration and, taking an egg from a clutch under a hen in another nest, transferred it to hers, retiring behind the arras to await results. It was very pretty to see her finding the treasure, talking to it, showing it proudly to her mate, then stepping carefully over it, lifting her feathered petticoats (as birds do) to watch her feet, and finally sitting down to cover it with her quivering wings.

Ten days later I watched the foster-parents helping the nestling off with its shell, and it grew to be the best bird of the year. After the whole colony had been returned to the owner, the odd one of the original eleven—a little green hen who was a confirmed spinster—pined for me and was brought back. She was a gifted little creature, and learned to say " Boy " quite distinctly, repeating it constantly like a parrot or tacking it on to the end of a twitter, so she too was something of a pioneer. She was a delightful companion but, except for this one accomplishment, less interesting than the hero of this little book. She slept at night inside a corner of my pillow-case which she regarded as

53

D*

her nest and defended against all comers, but she had no idea of keeping it clean and it had to be lined with a piece of washable material. As she died before my sparrow was born they never met.

I have nothing further to relate on the subject of my sparrow's affairs of the heart. Except in the breeding season, he was less demonstrative in his affection for me than in his cloistered youth. When, as was sometimes necessary, I left him for a few days in the care of a good neighbour who was also a friend of little birds, he was less spontaneous in his welcome on my return. He no longer flew to me like an arrow from a bow ; and if I had been absent for more than a week he would stand and stare, as if confused, before showing signs of recognition. But he made amends the next day by following me from room to room as if to make sure that I had not disappeared again.

I think I must have acquired a dual personality in his some-what bewildered consciousness, and my relationship to himself had become less clearly defined in whatever served him as a mind. As for his friends in the garden, no doubt he was fascinated and perhaps flattered by their attentions, and enjoyed their interest in him so long as they kept their place. If he ever experienced that strange inquietude that precedes the birth of love, as they fluttered up and down his window, it was soon forgotten. Once again the two great influences of heredity and environment had played their part in the development of his character and personality. This time, however, it had been a struggle, ending in a victory for the latter, though perhaps by only a narrow margin.

At the end of an exciting day he would still fly to me as in his earlier years, nestling close and looking up, with more expression than I could have believed possible in the eyes of a little bird, as if to say : " You are all I need and, after all, a boy's best friend is his mother."

CHAPTER FIVE

DECLINE AND FALL

There is little of interest to record in the life of my sparrow from the end of his sixth year until his serious illness and subsequent partial recovery in his twelfth, which is the main subject of this chapter. I give the details briefly as they may be of interest to students and breeders of birds.

After his delayed adolescence his character was formed, and his life being comparatively uneventful, his habits and behaviour remained more or less uniform. He was less interesting perhaps, except, of course, in the breeding-season; and I was no longer the only living thing that was of interest to him.

Even in the heyday of Spring, when he was vibrant with life and energy, his approach to me, though more rapturous, was also more guarded and secretive. The piano ceased to inspire him, except spasmodically, and our recitals together in the early mornings were discontinued, which may account for the deterioration in his song.

We moved again several times before the end of the war, and whenever he accompanied me, either by road or rail, he sat quietly in his swing and went to sleep until we arrived at our destination. I have never known a better traveller.

Towards the end of 1943 it became necessary for me to leave London and move to a well-known seaside resort in order to nurse my stepmother. I continued my Warden's duties so far as it was possible for me to do so ; but they were far less strenuous and exacting than they had been in London, and we were spared the terrors of the flying-bombs and rockets.

My sparrow's services as Professional Entertainer, if he could have been persuaded to give them, were no longer needed, but he was well-known at the various Posts to which I became attached, and he was visited with intense interest by some members of the Natural Science Society for which that town is famous, who watched his antics and listened to his vocal rhapsodies with amazement.

It was from one of these distinguished people that I first heard the story of the nightingales. These birds, he told me, paired for life and nothing but death ever permanently divided them. When the season of love was over, they separated and flew to a far distant land. The following Spring, about the middle of April, they returned and, faithful to their undying reciprocal love, they kept their tryst in the same hallowed spot in which they had first plighted their troth. The cock-bird arrived first and, in preparation for the return of the beloved, practised his love-song for seven days. At dawn on the eighth day (the Resurrection Day, the old man added significantly) his mate appeared and he sang to her as men and birds have sung since the sun first shone on the golden tresses of our mother Eve.

Can history or literature record for us a romance more exquisite than the love story of these birds ?

Like all truly great men, my sparrow was at home in any society, and became as famous in that little circle of distinguished men and women as he had been among the gallant Cockneys of his native city. Socially, I suppose, he had risen in the world ; but how superficial such distinctions seemed against the background of reality when in every city, town and hamlet in the land one could " walk with Kings nor lose the common touch."

The raids there, though severe, were mostly of the hit-and-run type and were often sudden and totally unexpected. One glorious summer afternoon I was seen by low-flying raiders who swooped out of a cloud and machine-gunned me as I was walking leisurely home from a tea-party to which my bird had also been invited. There was hardly time to realise what was happening, but someone shouted " Get down ! Get down ! " Quick as thought, I put the cage on the ground against a wall behind me and crouched over it, and in what seemed little more than a split second the danger had passed and the planes were out of sight. The sparrow preserved his usual equanimity and we reached home in safety. This was the last of our adventures together, and almost the last of all our adventures in this country, for after this came D-Day, the crossing of the Rhine, the Great Surrenders, the Fall of Berlin and the Death of Hitler.

And so Peace came at last. Meanwhile my stepmother had died and I began to turn my thoughts with longing towards my own home. The rush to the capital was like an avalanche, and it was some time before I could find anyone to remove me; but eventually we arrived in London and, as my bungalow had been repaired, we returned to it and settled down.

Contrary to my expectations, my little friend and comrade was quite unmoved by this happy return from exile. If he recognised the scenes of his childhood he gave no sign. The furniture was inspected, as it always was in new surroundings, to make sure it was the same that he had always known—but, when once he was completely satisfied on this point, there were no further comments.

Up to the beginning of his twelfth year he had never known a day's, or even a moment's, illness. He was a hardy little fellow and took his cold bath every day, even in the bitter winter of 1947, when he used to jump out after a good splash and go down my neck to get warm. His health was radiant, his spirits buoyant, and his strength such that I believe he could have fought any two of his wild relatives single-handed to a standstill.

Soon after his eleventh birthday, however, he began to have trouble with his feet, falling from his perch in the night, and to alarm me with occasional attacks of hysteria. Then, one morning he staggered out of his bath and fell on his side on the floor of his cage. I ran to pick him up and was distressed beyond measure to find him unconscious with his beak fixed open, though still breathing. Putting him down my neck for warmth, I rocked him gently to and fro, talking to him encouragingly as I swayed until, at the end of about half an hour, he stirred and was able to take a little warm milk and, later, to return to his cage.

It was a stroke, resulting in partial paralysis; and though he could still hop about and feed himself he was lop-sided, unsure of his balance, and seemed to have lost the use of his wings.

Having recently heard of a house-sparrow in an aviary who had had a similar seizure at the age of ten and had died soon after, I was extremely anxious about him. He was in a handsome cage at the time, nearly three feet high, and he persisted pathetically, but with magnificent courage, in climbing—with many tumbles—to his swing in its domed roof. That, as always, was to him a place of safety, a sanctuary second only to a hiding-place in my breast. It may be explained perhaps by the fact that the wild birds fly high when in danger to bough or roof-top which, in addition to offering them greater security, serves as an observation-post from which they can discover the cause of their alarm ; when they can no longer reach it, they know their end is near.

I nursed him as much as possible during the day inside my jumper, where he lay contented and at rest ; but I dare not have him in my bed at night for fear of crushing him, and he resolutely refused any other resting-place except his beloved swing. Hour after hour he would make the terrible ascent from the low perch on which I had placed him, panting and struggling until he reached it only to fall again, and these night-agonies were beginning to affect his heart. Something had to be done, and quickly ; so I bought a little long, low cage and, removing all but the two lowest perches, introduced him to his Eventide Home. He went in, as if with a sigh of relief, and adapted himself at once to a ground-floor flat. After all, as he soon discovered, there are advantages in sleeping close to the larder door, and for the next week at least something suspiciously like midnight celebrations appeared to be taking place under cover of darkness.

Yet, in spite of the improvement in his household arrangements, he was rapidly failing. He seemed to be suffering and in great distress ; and when I discovered that he had a stoppage I mixed a little olive oil with his food and went to look for a bird-doctor. In my heart I knew that he was dying and, like the Shulamite of old, I must go out and search for the man who could save the child ! After some hours of fruitless wandering I heard of a Veterinary Surgeon—Mr. T. Jenkinson Richardson, M.R.C.V.S., of Beckenham, Kent—who had made a special study of birds. I contacted him and he came at once. In his opinion the primary cause of the trouble was old age, but he suspected a growth.

The first thing to be done was to flatten the upper side of the perches, making them like a finger, so that the little feet could rest on them instead of curling round. This was an obvious relief, and I pass on the tip to anyone who has an aged bird. He advised greater warmth and complete protection from draught, so the cage was moved permanently from the window. To the medicine for the heart there was an immediate response; but the laxative gave no relief and the little patient grew rapidly worse. He was now losing his sight, the eyes becoming dull and quite flat, while his feathers, as the result of toxic absorption, began to peel off, not one by one, but like a jacket, until it looked as if he would become completely naked.

Then Mr. Richardson, for whose skill I can never be sufficiently grateful, tried him with Phthalylfulphathiazole—popularly known as M. and B. for Enteritis—and the result of the treatment with this drug was little short of miraculous. In less than a week a large fibrous mass had been expelled, the sight had begun to return, and the peeling of the feathers had ceased. There was now a faint hope in our hearts that we might save him; but, though the cause of the poison had been removed, he had no strength left with which to take the long, steep road to recovery. Almost helpless and very pitiful, though still courageous, and still turning his little head at the sound of my voice, he lay in the palm of my hand—a tiny bundle of bone and ragged feathers— and it looked as though we were beaten. "As a last hope," said Mr. Richardson, "try him with some champagne," and fetching a half-bottle from the nearest shop (to the intense amusement of the wine merchant) I gave him a teaspoonful neat. I say "gave," but the little fellow took all his nasty medicines without any fuss from a teaspoon. He evidently had the will to live and the sagacity to know that we were trying to help him.

The next morning—and let all Bacchanalians take note of it— there was a decided improvement in his condition. He had turned the corner. He had gained strength, too; and he held it, improved steadily and never looked back. The dose of champagne was given twice daily for a fortnight ; the sight was completely restored ; the feathers grew again on the bare places and he recovered his trousers and his Old School Tie. On Christmas Day he sat on my arm, shared my slice of the sacrificial turkey and drank with me to a happier year in the last of the champagne.

There was still a long way to go in spite of the miracle and, though cured of his complaint, he had not regained his youth. There was a serious lack of co-ordination between the wings, and the only use he could make of them was to help his feet, to let him down lightly when he fell, and to flutter when he asked to be fed. His balance was still precarious and he constantly fell on his back, calling quite cheerfully to me to come and set him on his feet again. He needed occupational therapy, as his doctor said. That was a little difficult to arrange, but he found his own solution of the problem and learnt to jump like a frog, becoming so expert that before long he could leap instantaneously into the air from his inverted position, turn a complete somersault and come down the right way up—surely a feat for a small bird even in the first blush of youth ! I fixed a perch across the first floor of his cage, and he turned his home into a gymnasium by jumping over this until the exercise had still further strengthened the muscles of his back and wings. He was an ingenious little creature and never gave way to depression or despair.

Diet, of course, had played its part in this spectacular recovery as well as drugs. In the place of egg and lettuce which, being too astringent, were forbidden, he was given Bemax with Glucodin, and a minute daily dose (about two drops) of cod-liver oil. My faith in vitamin foods and modern drugs, to say nothing of the delectable vintage, was greatly strengthened by their rapidly beneficial results on such a tiny patient, but all *he* remembered about them was that they were very nasty ! It was many weeks before he would touch milk again for fear of what it might contain. At the sight of a teaspoon, he would put his little head down and look away—just like a naughty child. I have never seen in any bird a gesture so expressive and so " nearly human."

CHAPTER SIX

THE LAST PHASE

After his illness my sparrow became a more faithful companion to me than he had been for many years, for, whatever his physical condition and his biological age, he had gone back to the days of his childhood. He had forgotten his old companions, the flutter of wild wings about his window and his Darien-view of the great world of Nature. When I lifted him to the fanlight for another glimpse of that enchanted land, he gave no sign of recognition and turned away, as if with a sigh. The sight of sparrows quarrelling in the garden no longer roused him to frenzy, or filled him with manly ambition to join their ranks and win his spurs in mortal combat. Never more, it seemed, proudly ruffling his bright plumage in the clear sunlight, would he listen with rapt and wondering attention to the songs of Spring, or lift so much as an eyebrow in mild astonishment at the pleading love-notes and amorous glances of lovelorn maids. Cupid, long-baffled and now defeated, shafts in quiver, had left him, never to return.

But he remembered none of these things, was content and had no regrets. He, too, had a song in his heart, not a refrain of haunting or consoling loveliness such as echoed in rare moments in the silence of my own, but one which I am tempted to believe brought him the same unfailing comfort and delight. All day he listened for the sound of my voice, and so long as he could hear it he had no fear. As for his immediate surroundings, he seemed to be totally unaware of them, and the re-arrangement of furniture or the introduction into his demesne of anything to which he was unaccustomed no longer released a flood of abuse or evoked the mildest of protests. Gone was the proud look, gone the fastidious air and the despotic will ; and in their place was the childlike suppliant attitude, as he crouched, half-lifting the little wings and pleading perpetually to be taken up and nursed. Once more he called to me and followed me from room to room like the eager fledgling of the days long passed. Once more I was all his little world; but he was happy, and that was all that mattered.

Gradually old age brought its disabilities as it must inevitably do to those of us who attain its distinction. He could now neither perch nor fly and, though he made the most exemplary efforts to keep himself clean and to preen his feathers, he was not very successful and had to be watched and tended continually. He was a perpetual astonishment to the Veterinary Surgeon who had never seen a small bird put up such a gallant fight against age and infirmity. " A canary," he said, " or a budgerigar would have given up and died long ago," but this mite with his indomitable will never gave up.

Instead he adjusted himself, apparently without repining and probably without remembering anything different, to his increasing limitations, and enjoyed to the full the measure of activity and the pleasures of life still available to him. What a lesson to those of us who are growing old, and how foolish we are to struggle perpetually to perform those accustomed duties that the young can do with so little effort while they look to us in vain for the counsel and understanding that only age can give. I have learnt many a lesson from my little bird that I trust will make me more reasonable, contented and helpful if I am granted extension of leave and live to be honoured with the gift of old age.

Unlike poor Susan, whose mind grew worse and worse as her body grew better, the sparrow's mental powers seemed to increase as the physical declined, and, for a time at least, he became I think more intelligent and adaptable than at any other time of his life. Nevertheless, he was becoming a great tie and, though he never complained, he must have felt the cold and discomfort of his hard, sanded floor when I was too far away to warm and cheer him. There is, I believe, a way out of every difficulty. I thought of how one Boy Scout had said to another, " The silly fool didn't know the thing couldn't be done so he went and did it." The word Scout gave me an idea.

Removing the two perches from his cage, as they were no

longer needed, I cut an old grey army-blanket into strips the size of his cage-floor with a flap at one end to roll over and make a little tent, and put one of them in his cage. Grit being essential to his health, I provided this for him in a food-dish placed among the usual ones, his kitchen thus being at one end and his tent-bed at the other. I then replaced him in his house and watched his reactions with great interest. He seemed to take in the situation at once and helped himself to sand and grit as if he had taken them from a dish all his life. As for his little tent, he showed as much pride and pleasure in it as a Boy Scout in his first camp. He peered into it, shook himself with delight and then rushed round to make sure that it possessed a back entrance. (Note the wild instinct that in many birds distrusts a nesting-site that can offer no second approach or way of escape). Finally, having been his own wise surveyor and approved the plans, he went inside and took possession. After a few happy mutterings quite different from anything I had ever heard before from him in his life, he fell asleep, warm, soft-couched and cosy, for over an hour.

From that time onwards, except that he still delighted in being nursed, he accepted the padded floor of his cage as the little world that contained, with the addition of my company, all that he desired or needed, and it became possible once more to leave him in safety and comfort for many hours. He benefited greatly from the warmth, and as the soft floor gave him confidence, he began to arrange his day, more or less regularly, into periods for food, rest and physical exercises. These last were quite astonishing !

No longer afraid of falling or of hurting his crippled feet on so soft a carpet, he turned the centre of his cage into a miniature Stadium for Olympic Games, jumping into the air or from one end to the other with a lettuce-leaf or a piece of apple in his beak—up and down, backwards and forwards—with surprising energy and enthusiasm. After that he invented what I can best describe as a game of Beak Ball, tossing a pea or other small object into the air, chasing after and retrieving it like a puppy with a ball. After about half an hour at these strenuous exercises he usually repaired to his kitchen, enjoyed a meal with the sharpened appetite of an athlete and returned to his tent for an hour's rest. True, as always, to his unerring instincts he kept this, as a good Scout should, always ready for inspection, and, so long as he had strength to move in and out, he never sullied it.

Unfortunately he discovered before long that he could roll up his carpet, beginning with the tent, and have great fun jumping over the roll ; but here for once he was unwise, for the exertion brought on a heart attack and I had to secure the carpet with tapes and put an end to that little game. He seemed now to be completely happy and, as the floor-covers could be taken out and washed with very little trouble, it became possible to keep him reasonably clean.

Although he could no longer perch he began, for the first time in his life, to use his deformed foot like a hand to steady his food-pots while he ate out of them. This, I think, and naturalists may agree with me, was a remarkable development and evidence of great intelligence in so old a bird. He gripped the rim of the pot quite firmly, and this new use for his weak foot no doubt arrested the atrophy of the muscles that his doctor feared as a result of his inability to perch. Later he used the right foot in the same way while standing on his left and, working them more or less alternately, so kept his balance. More remarkable still, on occasions when hopping seemed too great an exertion, he quite definitely walked or at least waddled, using first one foot and then the other. I should be intensely interested to know if any ornithologist or bird-watcher has ever seen a sparrow walk.

Unfortunately I was unable to obtain a photograph of this phenomenon, although in the picture where he is seen enjoying " bread and milk for supper " a claw of his left foot is just visible gripping the pot while his right holds my supporting finger. Indeed, he became so intelligent with his feet that, if he had been more sure of his balance, I can almost believe that I could have taught him to shake hands with me.

This was not the last of the surprises he had to spring on me. Suddenly abandoning his Olympic Games, he took to hoarding food, much as a squirrel does, though without any attempt to hide it. He dragged or carried peas, cherries and other delicacies into a corner where he could reach them without much effort from his bed. Curious to see if he could be induced to store these in some kind of larder, I made a little outhouse of grey felt and placed them inside ; but he didn't approve of this at all and, after pulling some of them out, he ignored it and I took it away. A few weeks later he gave up this curious habit altogether and appeared to have forgotten it.

Wisely, too, this little person—for it becomes increasingly difficult to me to think of him as a mere bird—chose his diet, eliminating from his lavish menu everything that he considered unsuitable or indigestible. He drank less water and, except for bread-and-milk and Bemax, lived almost exclusively on soft fruit and strained vegetables. As a result of this restraint upon his appetite, I was soon able to discontinue the daily medicine that I feared had become a permanent necessity. Truly the wisdom with which Nature has endowed her " irrational " children is past belief ! Perhaps, if she were able to modify the severity of her winters and to forbid the strong to prey upon the weak, birds in a world without enemies might reach a ripe old age, find their own solution to their difficulties and live in their own little Homes for the Aged until they sank peacefully into their last sleep. It is mere idle speculation, of course, but interesting.

He slept now at night, not like a bird, lightly with head folded into the wing, but like a child wrapt in deep slumber apparently dreamless and full of rest and refreshment. I know this for a fact since I sat up for several nights to watch him. He just fell asleep in my hand in whatever position he happened to be in at the time, as a child does on the floor or in its nurse's arms. Sleep, that gentle, kindly attendant of the very old and the very young, came thus each night to the sparrow. Then I would slip him gently into his little bed, and there would be no sound and no stirring of the grey tent-sides until seven o'clock the next morning.

What I missed most of all was his song, and what a miss it was ! It had been my pride and joy for so many years but he never sang again after his stroke. Indeed, I believe his memory had been wiped clean of every experience between his childhood and the moment of that calamity, but I shall have more to say on that very interesting subject at the end of this chapter. He still talked a great deal and often carried on quite a conversation with me from his bed. What it was intended to convey I have no idea, but if he were not a philosopher he certainly behaved as though his tiny head contained the wisdom of the ages.

This was indeed the last phase of a life rich in experience and achievement, and it was not without interest or even without its triumphs. And so he came, as it were, to an Indian Summer of untroubled calm, life's battles over, its problems solved, its perplexities forgotten.

It occurred to me suddenly, as I sat at work on the final chapter of this short biographical study, that much of what I had written might seem incredible without concrete evidence of some good illustrations. I had been bird-watching for nearly a dozen years at very close quarters and foolishly had not secured a single photograph. My sparrow's life, from my point of view, had begun as an experiment and had ended as a revelation; but a camera was needed to convince my readers that what I said was true. If only he could be induced to illustrate his own life!

As a forlorn hope I made an appointment with Kenneth Gamm of Gordon Chase Ltd., Bromley, Kent, to visit the house and give him a sitting. I felt he would be more at ease in his own home than in a strange studio, but I had very little hope of the success of my project, for he had become so nervous since his illness that he usually ran into my dress, more like a mouse than a bird, at the approach of a stranger. Still the experiment was worth trying, and once again he was to surprise us. Not only was he completely without fear, but showed himself eager and willing to do whatever was required of him. The two tall young men, the queer camera with its mysterious black hood and its three long straddling legs creeping furtively nearer, and the glaring arc-lights above his head had no terrors for him. There was no need for bribery; no coaxing and no camouflaging on my part and no hesitancy on his. He went steadily through all the little tricks, and in their correct order, that he had learned in the Kindergarten and had not practised or even once performed for over six years, and he crowned this superb performance (for an old and ailing bird) by lying on his back to " die for Queen and Country ! " It was astonishing ! The whole sitting took less than half an hour, only two plates were wasted and the photographs, with some that were added later, are reproduced in this book. Unfortunately, they cannot give so much as a hint of his former beauty, for tattered, dingy and draggled, with eyes that had lost their lovely beaded rims, he was no longer a Beau Nash among the sparrows. But they show at least that his faculties were unimpaired, that he was still capable of expression and, above all, that he possessed the gift of memory.

There was a remarkable coincidence that I would like to mention in connection with the picture called " The Daily Reading " where he is shown gazing quietly, as if in thought, at the page of a small devotional classic known as " Daily Light." The book, chosen solely on account of its size, had been taken from a pile of others and opened at random on the spur of the moment. After the photograph had been developed I found that the words to which his little beak was pointing were these : " Are not two sparrows sold for a farthing, yet not one of them falls to the ground without your Father ? "—a statement that embodies, perhaps, the most astounding revelation of the value to the Creator of the individual personality of the creature in the pages of Holy Writ. This, then, was the portrait of a sparrow, ignorant and insignificant, yet unconsciously a greater teacher than Karl Marx. This, it seemed, was to be his little sermon, his farewell message to doubting and perplexed humanity ; and as such I pass it on. Fear not, therefore ! Ye are of more value than many sparrows.

It was now the end of March, 1952, nearly seven years since the long-looked-for day that proclaimed the end of the conflict in Europe. Hitler was dead and to many of us he was scarcely a memory ; but I and my small companion for one brief moment had gone back together to the nights of the Black-out and the Blitz. The scene in my little kitchen faded from my mind, and

I was back once more in the old Warden's Post with my comrades watching a fledgling sparrow on the table beside the helmets, the gas masks and the inevitable pot of tea, while he entertained us as we waited for the " Banshee Wailings."

How can I explain this phenomenal resurgence of such an aged bird, this sudden and unexpected reversion to the memories and activities of his youth ? I have pondered over it a great deal. Was this tiny creature, a mere insignificant sparrow, like very old people, " living in the past " and, though conscious of the immediate present, remembering only the early and forgetting the intervening years ? I must leave the question unanswered as I bring this simple story to its conclusion but, if my hypothesis is correct, then the mind of a little bird is of greater interest than ornithologists have so far guessed.

After he had sat to the photographer for the third time he seemed to tire of the ordeal, and I thought it unfair to make further demands upon his patience. Almost as though he knew that his life's work was now completed—as indeed it was—he retired from all unnecessary activities and rested most of the day dozing in the doorway of his tent. His sight was failing once more and he was losing his feathers again disastrously, this time without being able to replace them, the tail and wing-tips becoming brittle and breaking off. His doctor suggested a Hormone tablet that might stimulate the growth of new plumage but, as he was happy and well protected from cold, he agreed with me that it might be kinder to let Nature take its course and not to attempt to prolong his life beyond his ability to enjoy it.

He still delighted in his hairpin and often sat with it in his beak like an old man with his pipe, or laid it, like a trophy, at the door of his tent. When he dies I think it should be buried with him ; and if, after that sad event, I embroidered a Banner or designed for him a Coat-of-Arms or a Tablet of Memory, I should emboss it with the device of a Golden Hairpin as a symbol of a little life that was often astonishingly human—the twin points signifying courage and contentment.

What would be the end of him, I wondered ? Would he fall asleep like a tired child, suddenly and without awakening, as he

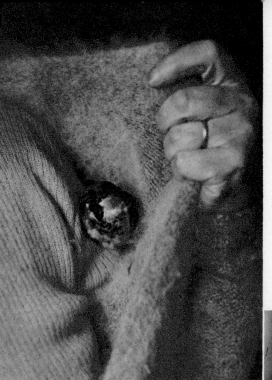

The Secret Nest

*Now I am an old man
I like bread and milk
for supper*

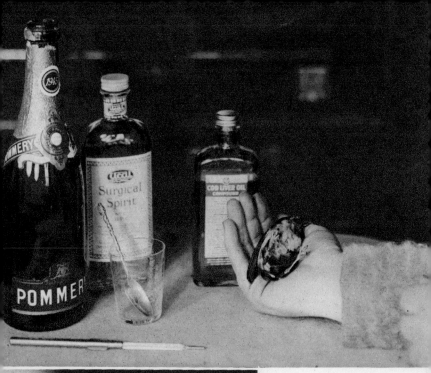

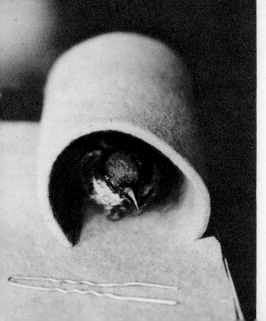

Waiting for the doctor.
Is he coming soon ?

So now I will bid you
goodbye

nestled at my neck, or would he die peacefully in his tent like a tiny warrior who, though a cripple from birth, had fought without faltering through life's long day and come at last to his well-won rest ? Only the future could tell, but the shadows were lengthening and that long day was surely drawing to its close.

EPILOGUE

—

The Winter months have left us without regret. April is on the threshold, but she comes without laughter, warily and with a muffled tread. The almond-tree (or wake-tree as it was once called) stretching out its hands, laden with fresh beauty to awake the earth, has flowered and faded; for a bitter wind has chilled the ardour of the Spring, and the snow falls thickly on lawn and covert. Outside, on the frozen but hospitable window-ledge, the sparrows fight for crumbs; but my small companion pays no heed to them. He is more fortunate than they, for cold and hunger are unknown to him, and I like to think that he has been as happy.

It seems he may outlast the Summer but I doubt if another Spring will quicken his little pulse, for he has the appearance of a very old bird. I hope that his departure will be sudden, for to hasten it would be like murdering a friend. When he goes from me I have faith enough to believe that I shall see him again.

I have a fancy, fantastic enough perhaps, and one that many people might ridicule, that when death comes to the beasts and birds they are not alone, but that some spirit or influence, whether of animal or angel I know not, comforts and sustains them at the end. The instinct that prompts them to seek solitude in their last hours may have a deeper significance than we know. However that may be, we are assured on the Highest Authority, and in no uncertain language, that no sparrow falls without the knowledge of the Father of Love. I have confidence that mine will not be an exception.

He is sitting on my wrist as I write, chirping happily, knowing nothing of what the future may have in store for him and caring nothing for the present so long as he is with me.

In a final assessment of his values as friend and companion I will use the past tense, for he is a child again, desiring only to be warmed and fed. His character, except for his fierce little temper and his jealousies, was without fault. He was never destructive, and never greedy though always ready to be fed. An opportunist, as all sparrows are, yet he never stole and never helped himself to anything that was not offered to him. He was neither cunning nor deceitful, and he had none of the hesitancy of the canary nor the solemn deliberation of the budgerigar. Gay, eager and impulsive, he knew exactly what he wanted to do and was not easily turned from his purpose. His ability to adapt himself to all circumstances within the narrow limits of his life was consistent, and his courage and cheerfulness, even in illness and infirmity, have never failed. His faithfulness to me was never seriously in doubt.

His gift of song may, or may not, have been almost the only one ever bestowed upon his species. Other sparrows may have sung in captivity but (save for the little friend of Catullus) I have never heard of them. If they have, their song must have been different from his. It would be strange indeed if the Divine Muse, pressing heedlessly through a crowd of chattering sparrows in her search for nightingale and woodlark, on a sudden impulse touched him and him only as she passed. It may be that without the piano he would never have sung ; but at least he has proved that such an accomplishment is possible to his kind, and might even delight us from the roof-tops if there were less quarrelling and chatter.

In intelligence I do not think he was outstanding. I have known cleverer birds. His interest and charm lay in his ability to reveal his wild nature, through the medium of his unusual surroundings, in a language that a human mind could share and understand. And in this perhaps he was unique.

My Sparrow died on August 23rd, 1952, four months after this little book was written. He was nearly blind, though his hearing was still acute. Too weak to stand, though he made two gallant attempts to do so, he settled himself quietly in my warm hand and lay motionless for several hours. Suddenly he lifted his head, called to me in his old intimate way and was gone. He had lived twelve years, seven weeks and four days, and was courageous, intelligent and apparently conscious to the end. The cause of death was extreme old age.

His remains—and what a tiny morsel of tattered feathers was all that was left of him—repose in a small Hoptonwood tomb sacred to the memory of

CLARENCE

THE FAMOUS AND BELOVED SPARROW

———